Published by
Chihuahua Books Oü
Narva mnt 5
10117 Tallinn
Estonia

ISBN-13:
978-1726443180

ISBN-10:
1726443183

A children's book by

www.chihuahua.dog
publishing

ONCE UPON A TIME THE PERFECT SOCIALIST WORLD EXISTED…

100 years ago the world saw socialism happen for the first time. Everybody was equal in that promised land. People did not worry about making decisions because decisions were made for them by the big government. Everything was owned by everybody. To each was given according to what the government thought they needed, and from each it was taken what the government thought they were capable of giving.

- 'Papa, have things always been like this?'
- 'Like what, little Alyosha?' -replied father.
- Good and fair and happy?' -he responded.
- 'Before we were not equal, now we have a government
for the likes of us, not born in big palaces'

Alyosha's father remembers a time when
the people were not equal,
where the government didn't strive
to make the lives of all the people better.

Russia was an agricultural nation before
the great revolution and most people
were engaged in farming, however
the tools and methods they had were very old
and this life was tough.

In these days, many things were considered
a luxury and were not in reach of a boy.

- Why are you not going to your family, Aleksandr? —the farmer asked.
- I must work more to feed them, Boris —replied Alexei's father.

3

It was in those days when the world saw the birth of socialism
and with it the promise of equality.
In theory, socialism would unburden the people from having
to make decisions for themselves as the government
would makes those decisions for them.

Socialism was said to be based on a noble idea: that
people should own the means of production and not be
slaves to the capitalist class that previously owned them.

But not all that glitters is gold. In order to organize such
a society, the government had to decide who was to work, where
and for how long. Sure, some saw that ideal world as a big relief,
as they would be unburdened from thinking for themselves.

- Look Aleksandr! I harvest more food
with the tractor! —said the farmer.
- And I can make more tools with
this machine, Boris! —his friend replied.

People like Aleksander were upset because he would see the town's people work hard, wearing worn down clothes and having haggard faces, and yet the capitalists owning the tractors and machines would be wearing the finest clothes and eating the finest foods every night. Aleksandr and many others thought it was not fair.

Boris was told that while he sweated in the field,
the owner of the tractor was in bed,
reading the newspaper and eating fancy food.

Of course such discontent caused people to dream about progress. But progress was slow and those wanting the "great socialist revolution" would constantly badger farmers like Boris and factory workers like Aleksandr, poisoning their hearts with hatred.
They would ask them "why should you work harder and longer just to put profits in a capitalist's pocket?"
Why could they not work less, see their family more and spend more time at home?
-the socialist agitators would ask the workers.

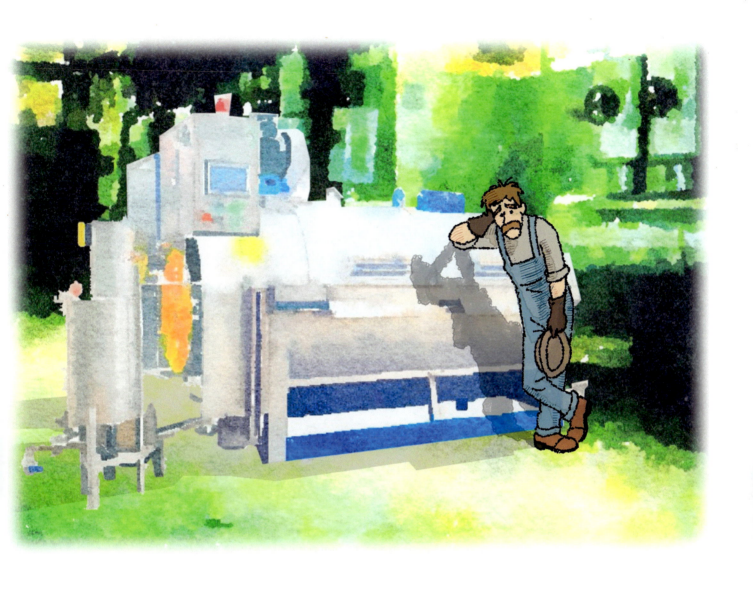

People like Aleksandr were told:
"If you make more things, why not more money?"

Before the great revolution ushered in a great
industrialization, there were many more machines
in the factories and more tractors in the field
due to capitalist investment, despite the profits
not being even. Also, the state was not protecting
the workers like Aleksandr and often the
capitalists were in cahoots with the state.

That is why in those days people started to organize
and try to change things democratically.
Whenever the government crushed those attempts,
the socialists gained more and more reputation
among workers, because socialists kept telling
workers that democracy was not the answer and
socialism had to be brought about via
a violent revolution.

Suddenly, everybody with money became the enemy.

It was a very tense time. There were good and bad
bureaucrats, compassionate capitalists and others not
so much, peaceful workers, and then, of course,
the socialists, who were always angry and wishing
for a revolution. These socialists saw capitalists as
the oppressors of the workers and thought that
the workers had to keep the profits of their labor.

In those days there were people who sincerely
thought that workers and capitalists could work
together as they each had different skills and
things to offer. Even thought there were differences
between them, some thought that there were ways
of solving the imbalances in a peaceful manner.
And their hopes were based on the improving lives
of people like Aleksandr and his family, who were now
working with machines bought by the capitalists
instead of with their hands!

But at the end change was too slow and hate won.
The socialists had planted too many seeds of resentment
and, instead of trying to change things
through democracy and dialogue, they
started a violent revolution.

The socialist revolution was underway.

A lot of these ideas came from a man called Karl Marx, a German who believed that people would eventually own everything and that the capitalist class would die away. Even though socialism and communism are not the same thing, they are both opposed to capitalism, and communism is an extreme form of socialism –because whomever has power tends to want more of it and socialism usually tends towards communism.

They both adhere to the principle that economic resources should be collectively owned and controlled by a central organization, and differ in who makes the decisions: the collective as a whole or a few leaders representing them? Whatever the merits of their ideas, the revolutionaries that came after Marx used those same ideas to justify killing the capitalists and then proclaimed that they would do the same all over the world.

Karl Marx had a lot of ideas,
some of which had huge consequences.

When the socialists won by violent means, at the beginning everything went well because the tools and factories they stole from the capitalists were still in good order.

The government was now in charge where private capitalists used to be and began to plan everything. This led to the government planning what people did and how they did it. If the government decided they needed new farmers in the east, it would compel people to move east and become farmers, even if they wanted to do something else and they were not good at farming. Those that wanted to be footballers or musicians had to put their dreams on hold. People accepted this initially though because they felt that it was a sacrifice for the greater good.

When everything is planned, even YOU are planned!

Not everything was o.k. though. Back then in Europe there were two types of socialists. On one side, the international socialists, who followed Karl Marx and wanted socialism everywhere, who believed that the working class were brothers wherever they were and needed to band together to overthrow the capitalist class. They believed in tearing down borders as capitalists could control people more easily when countries were separated by borders. On the other hand, there were the national socialists, who thought brotherhood came from belonging to the same national group rather than work. Both types of socialists were collectivists but their focus was different: international socialists thought solidarity came through belonging to the working class while national socialists thought solidarity came through race.
They both wanted power, couldn't live side by side, and so they went to war.

Two types of socialism went to war
to figure out which one was "best."

After many years of cruel battles, the international socialists won the war against the national socialists. Countries like America and Great Britain loved freedom and even though they disagreed with many aspects of socialism, they allied with the international socialists because the national socialists were considered more dangerous. Both types of socialists wanted similar things: state-controlled healthcare, education, media, industry, banking, and religious expression.

The individual person was not important for them, only the group. But the American and British heroes had to make a choice in the war, and back then they did not know about the crimes of the international socialists, just the crimes of the national socialists, so they fought together against a common enemy.

The international socialists won with help from America.

After the war came peace. Or kind of.
The socialist paradise looked to the outside world as if it was the future of humanity.
Many people around the world wanted their own countries to become socialist! What was not to like? The socialists had won a big war, their industries and farms were full of supplies, and everybody was apparently equal.
The leaders of the government of the socialist paradise started to claim that they were materially and morally superior, even when compared to their allies in the war!
So they started competing against freedom loving countries like America and Great Britain, trying to convince their workers to start a revolution too.

The workers of the socialist paradise returned home as heroes.

The socialist war heroes returned home to their families.
At home they had to immediately get to work. You see, when
everybody has to get the same, then everybody has to work,
whether they want it or not. This was different for the big
government bosses running the socialist paradise, of course,
as they were busy planning everything for the common good
and, therefore, they had to be rested, well fed, and
comfortable in order to lead the socialist paradise.
But, hey, the heroes didn't mind at that time.
They had won the war! They had saved their families from the
other socialists, and they could be proud of their effort.
They didn't notice how the ideas of Marx were progressing
and, as it happens, socialism was converting
into communism: the rule of a few over the many.

Alexei was very proud of his father, Aleksandr,
because he was a hero.

Everybody though that everything was going to be fine now. Sadly, life was about to change for the heroes and for many others in the socialist paradise. Folks like Aleksandr, his wife, and their little Alyosha were about to be visited during the night, by surprise, and not by nice people. Nobody expected it and that only made it much more terrifying. Armed with their uniforms, badges, and guns, members of the socialist secret police starting to show up at their houses and arrest them without any motive.

The secret police started entering homes and arresting people in the middle of the night.

And just like that, the big government running the socialist
paradise started taking people away from their families.
Without explanation! No due process! No justification!
In total, during those years they took away millions of people.

Imagine if one night there is a van in your street, taking away
your friends That's scary, isn't it? Even though both socialism
and communism consider capitalism a threat to equality,
socialism eventually gives way to communism and for
communists the goal is to destroy capitalism completely.
So, the socialist paradise was turning power hungry and their
leaders, who lived in comfort and not like workers,
were turning more and more paranoid.

Fathers, mothers, young and old. They took them away.

That is when many in the socialist paradise started to realize what was really happening. After being taken away from their families they were interrogated and mistreated. In our world, the West, people are innocent until proven guilty by a court of law, but it wasn't like that in the socialist paradise.
There were no trials at all or at least not real ones, you know, with a fair judge and a jury. Also, the law did not apply to protect the life and integrity of those being detained, especially if the big government gave the order.
The "common good" was above the rights of the individual, therefore every abuse could be justified if it was for the good of the collectivity.

This is called torture, but back then it was called "social justice."

After days, weeks or months of interrogation, the millions of people taken away from their families started to be moved into locked train wagons.
Aleksandr, the war hero, was among them. It was cold and they were all sent to even colder places, far away from any town or village. Where were they taking them and why?

They were sending them to places known as gulags and many years later the whole world would discover that the socialist paradise was, in reality, full of gulags.

People were sent to gulags: forced labor camps.

People like Aleksandr, the war hero who had helped save the socialist paradise during the war, never saw their family ever again. They were all placed in cold cells and given little or no food at all, and whenever they got sick there was no doctor to help them.

Aleksandr and the many others imprisoned in the gulag were forced to work, either cutting wood, mining minerals or carrying heavy bags all day, every day.

As time went by, Aleksandr started to meet the other people who were, like him, imprisoned in those gulags.

And he was about to discover that he was not the only one who was there despite not having done anything wrong.

Your freezer at home is at zero Fahrenheit.
Those cells were even colder.

For example, at the gulag Aleksandr met old farmers, many of them old women whose "crime" had been to hide one sack of grain so they could eat during the winter –instead of giving it all to the big government.
Remember the beginning of the socialist paradise? Yes, they kicked the capitalist class so everyone would own everything, right?
So now, because everything was the property of everyone, one sack of grain not surrendered to the government was considered theft! Theft from the people!
Even though that poor woman had worked extra time to save a bit more for the winter, by saving that little grain to survive, that woman had betrayed the working class and become an enemy:
a capitalist.

Old women who stashed more grain than permitted were considered enemies.

At the gulag Aleksandr also met artists. What was their crime? Well, there were several types. Some artists were arrested and sent to the gulag because they had made a joke about the socialist paradise and nobody was allowed to joke about it!
It was a paradise after all, remember? Other artists were punished for owning "forbidden books", mostly talking about capitalism, the system of freedom and individuality that existed in places like America. A few other artists were sent to the gulag because they had friends outside of the socialist paradise. In those cases the big government considered them "contaminated" with exotic ideas, you know, like individualism, life, liberty, and the pursuit of happiness. Socialists don't like dissenters so they punish anyone who dares to think different, you see?
That is why at the gulag they also sent Christians.
Socialists hate religion because it gives people hope and makes them realize that they are special, loved, and not part of a machine

Artists who joked about socialism were considered enemies too.

Aleksandr also discovered that millions of people living in the socialist paradise were spies. They eavesdropped on their neighbors, friends, colleagues, and even family.
They informed against them to the secret police for the crime of "betraying the working class." Sometimes they did it because they hated those they accused and they knew the secret police would take them away.
In other cases the accusers sincerely believed that they lived in the perfect society and anyone with a different opinion was a "class enemy."
Nobody trusted anyone because you could be accused of being like the artist, or the old farmer lady, and then sent to the gulag.

The secret police was everywhere, eavesdropping on everyone.

And then there was the forced and unpaid work at the gulag.
Millions of "class enemies" of the socialist paradise were forced
to work for free, with little rest and almost no food.
The "economic miracle" of the socialist paradise was actually
thanks to slavery!
When the machines and tools that they had stolen from the
"capitalist enemies" broke down, the socialist paradise created
goods and products at the gulags, making it appear as if their
system was really working well.
That is, of course, until those people in the gulags started to die
from cold, hunger and disease, reducing the production to
almost nothing.

People don't like to be forced to work for free, it seems.

That was the moment when Aleksandr, like many other gulag prisoners, realized that something was not just wrong with the socialist paradise, but that the so-called paradise itself was a lie!

Aleksandr loved his country and he believed in the dream of creating the perfect society. He even had fought a war to defend it! Why was he being punished for having opinions? Also, if he was "working class" according to the socialists, why was he forced to work for free and why was he oppressed by the big government, which supposedly was also "working class"? Wasn't the "capitalist class" the real enemy? Weren't they all supposed to be equal? Wasn't socialism supposed to free them from oppression?

Aleksandr had a sudden realization.

So people started slowly to wake up to reality. Like many others in the gulag, Aleksandr realized that what you do for work, or whether you have very little or a lot of money, doesn't make you identical or different to others or a "class". Men, women, young, old, rich, poor, accountants, farmers, musicians, teachers, or drivers, it doesn't matter, people are not their work or what they possess. He realized that the exterior appearance is not what makes people diverse but what is inside: values, knowledge, kindness and character. The "class war" was a lie invented to divide and create conflict. That isn't to say that things were fairer or more just before the revolution but that one tyranny had replaced another.
A society in conflict, divided in groups, is easier to control and, those who control a divided society have a great life just "planning" the economy. That is why the socialist leaders had a great life while the rest of the country suffered.

People have different dreams, personalities, opinions, and talents.

What the leaders of the socialist utopia had done, Aleksandr realized, was to try to make robots out of people and that, despite effort or talent, everybody had to get the same outcome. This is unfair because the only fair thing is to get what one deserves. Surely if somebody works harder or smarter, it is fair to get more benefits from that effort. And it is unfair that someone who does nothing gets also the same as someone who works. Aleksandr noticed also that the leaders of the government running the socialist paradise lived like the old "capitalist class", the "enemy": very comfortably. Where was the equality?

Equality of opportunity is not the same as equality of outcome.

What the agitators selling the socialist paradise to the masses had told Aleksandr and his comrades about the "capitalist class" was exactly what they were guilty of doing now. Aleksandr realized that people are not robots but have different dreams and talents. For example: some are good making music, others are good playing sports and then others are good at investing money.

He saw that they are not enemies among each other but, instead, when people work together they make their dreams come true and everybody wins.

A good musician making a good song is like a good investor making a good business. And, in that example, if both work together, they can make music that people want to buy and they all profit from, not the least those who buy the music, who can listen to what they want, not what the government tells them they are "authorized " to listen to.

Socialist bureaucrats became the
true class enemies of the people.

In the 1950s the people living in the socialist paradise started to wake up. The "working class" was hungry, exploited, and dreaming about freedom. This made the socialist leaders nervous! The slaves in the gulags were dying and therefore producing less and less. Also, the countries where socialism had been "exported" into by force, sometimes by means of military brutality, wanted to be free and had started to protest against their oppressive socialist rulers. The worst of all for the big government running the socialist paradise was that the free countries, like America or Great Britain, were doing very, very well, showing that socialism wasn't necessarily the better system.

"If socialism is superior, why is it failing?" they asked themselves

Yes, the free world was doing great! And it was doing great at the same time that the socialist world was crumbling into pieces. In places like America the workers did not work like in the gulags but instead had job security, good pay, and free time to do with their lives what they enjoyed most. They were saving money and, if they worked hard and learned new skills, were being promoted to better jobs. How was that possible if, according to the socialists, all that capitalists wanted was to exploit the workers?

A happy worker clocking in, it could be tough
but this wasn't a gulag

Furthermore as a consequence of the improving conditions of workers in the free world, people were having the chance, if they worked smart and saved money, to send their kids to university in order to study whatever subject they dreamed about -unlike in the socialist paradise, where the big government ordered them what to study and what to do. This allowed the next generation in the free world to have more tools in order to gain social mobility, which means having a better life than one's parents.

It's nicer when you study what you want,
not what the government tells you to.

Also, and unlike in the socialist paradise, in the free world people were free to start their own business and keep their profits. Even when a business started small, like a lemonade stand or a small band, freedom means that with the right attitude and teaming up with other entrepreneurs (like the "capitalist class" that was expelled from the socialist utopia) the business can become big and give jobs to many people.

Hey, with the right attitude and hard work, anyone can become what the socialists call the "enemy": the "capitalist class"! In the socialist paradise that was not allowed because nobody could "exploit" others and of course the government knew what was better for the collective, so they crushed any symptom of individualism.

Only in a free society you can reach
your dream of being your own boss.

And, believe it or not, what the youth in the oppressive socialist paradise yearned for the most was music, especially Rock and Roll. Yes Rock and Roll! In a free world, it is an option for a youngster to say "I am going to make music" and then start a band. Sometimes that band becomes huge. And the youngsters living in socialism envied that aspect of the free world, the freedom to rebel and express their feelings through rock music. Suddenly, all over the socialist paradise, young people started to wake up and demand freedom from the oppression of socialism.

Keep On Rockin' in the free world!

And that is when the situation went out of control in the socialist paradise. The countries that had been "converted by force" into socialism didn't want to be a part of it anymore. Therefore, they started to protest peacefully against the oppression they suffered. In 1956 the students of Hungary took to the streets to demand freedom. The leaders of the socialist paradise, because they believed that people valuing the individual and their own freedom above the collective were committing high treason against socialism, decided to roll in the tanks and crush the protests. Over 3,000 people died.

Socialism, so good that it has to be imposed by force.

The big government of the socialist paradise was not able to hide the news of what had happened in Hungary.
Also, to make things more complicated for them, the leader of the socialist paradise, a little bald man named Nikita, gave a speech during those days recognizing that bad things had been done in the name of socialism, including the disappearance of dissidents and the encouragement of a celebrity cult around the big government leaders, the same ones who claimed to be "working class", equals and friends of the people.

"Yes, maybe we did some naughty things" they confessed.

The socialist paradise was in reality a hell on earth. Aleksandr, the war hero, who had survived the hunger and forced labor of the gulag, was fed up from all the abuse. Therefore, he started to write about the horrors he and others had experienced in the gulag. Since it was illegal to criticize the government in the socialist paradise, every page he wrote was hidden in parts by many different people and taken out of the country. When his book was finally published the whole world was in shock. So many people had believed that socialism was indeed a paradise so when the truth came out their entire belief system crumbled.

Thanks to Aleksandr the world finally
heard about the horrors of the gulags.

Many of those who were brokenhearted by the unmasking of the socialist paradise as a true hell were university teachers who wanted to convert their free countries into "socialist paradises." They were members of the local socialist parties and their reputation was built as "bad boys" or rebels who knew a lot about socialism. But now socialism was dying! Remember Karl Marx? Well, some of those university teachers also knew nothing else but his teachings, for example. They thought that everything was based on power struggles between "classes" and that oppression was at the center of existence. And now they felt lost because their "idol" was wrong and their "socialist paradise" was a lie.

Sacre bleu, mon ami! Le socialisme est mort

To make things worse for those university teachers who had made a comfortable living off teaching and talking about Marx and socialism, after the debacle of the socialist paradise the world started to discover its true cost. In total, socialism killed millions of people, some by being exploited in working camps like the gulag, some others by lack of food, and most were shot for being "enemies of the people". Socialism had failed not only economically but also morally.

The legacy of socialism: equality in death.

But the socialist professors (who by the way lived comfortably enjoying the fruits of capitalism) refused to give up. Their reputations were at risk and some had started to murmur that they were nothing but charlatans. They had to come with a new idea, and quick, before losing their jobs. It wasn't an easy task, though. Capitalism had demonstrated that people weren't defined by what they do ("class") but, instead, by the content of their character. Moreover, all the people trying to escape the socialist paradise had demonstrated that people love freedom. Also, that life is unequal but that it is o.k. as long as the rules of the game are fair. Most importantly, the wealth created in free societies had shown that capitalists and workers were not enemies but teammates, and that the value of a product is not determined by the amount of work put into it but by the price that a free market is willing to pay for it.

When all you have is a hammer, everything looks like a nail.

So, those Marxist teachers went back to basics: envy! Yes, envy. You see, socialism is built on envy. For example, when you see a kid in your school who has better tennis shoes than you, you have three options: One, you do nothing because you also have other nice things and, hey, the brand of tennis shoes isn't that important, right? Two, you start walking dogs or mowing the lawn for your neighbors so you save some extra money and buy yourself nicer tennis shoes. And, third, you steal those kids' tennis shoes or destroy them so he doesn't have nicer shoes than you. Socialism is like option number three. It exploits envy and resentment, forcing equality of outcome on everyone.

Socialism's big challenge: When everything is good,
how can you make it go bad?

But because socialism had failed and capitalism had succeeded, socialists in the free world started to poison the minds and hearts of people again. They called it "inequality". And they started whispering to people who had a good life: "Sure, you have a good life, but have you seen how better others have it? Do you think they work as hard as you do?" It was, just as many years ago, the silly idea that the "oppressor class" worked less and value came from the amount of work put into something, not about effort and being smart and saving.

"Yes, you are doing well, but...
why are others doing better than you?"

Once those nostalgic socialists had planted the seed of envy, it was time to resuscitate class warfare. But how could they do that if capitalism had triumphed by making workers not oppressed but richer? They came up with the idea of "identity politics". Just like Karl Marx had said: "you are what you do (a worker or a capitalist)", the modern socialists came up with a variation of that: you are your tribe or group, and you are oppressed by capitalism in general just by being different or "disadvantaged". So, according to these socialists, people act, think, feel, and talk only according to their group characteristic: sex, skin color, age, ethnicity, or sexual orientation. They started to tell people that they don't think and decide freely but are defined by their "identity". Their goal was to create again the idea of oppression and war between "classes" of people.

The "new" socialists love racism
because it divides people in "tribes".

Once the socialists convinced people that those who had more did not work hard for it, and that it wasn't allowed to think independently but only according to one's sex, skin color, ethnicity, etc., it was time to push further: "capitalist pigs" not only exploited people for "being different" but also did it by destroying the planet. So the "socialist teachers" started inventing that capitalism had worked only because it destroyed the world.

Nature, too, is oppressed by capitalism, so say the socialists.

Facts did not matter to socialists. Their entire discourse is about feelings. The socialist teachers who were defeated before, when socialism failed in making people happier and freer, were back with a vengeance. They divided people into tribes instead of uniting them, they planted resentment in people's hearts. And they lied. In 1980 half of the world was living in absolute poverty but now it is far less poor, and with such advances other good things happened too: less children died of hunger, less wars occurred, and people started to live longer! But they didn't tell people that. They started teaching people that everything is relative (even morality!) and that there is no such thing as truth, just opinions. Also, they started teaching that everything is about power and that the world is divided between oppressors and oppressed.
And just like in the days of the gulag, they mocked and con-demned Christianity again, so people would lose hope and stop to see themselves as unique and loved individuals.

If you make people angry they stop thinking
and start "feeling". Bad choice.

Why were people believing those lies again? The answer is that freedom is beautiful but is not easy. When you are free to think, say, believe, and do whatever you want, as we have in the free world, there are consequences too. And only mature people can handle consequences. Picture this: let's say that you are free to come and go from your parents' house and they trust you. One day you decide to play soccer inside the living room and you kick the ball and break a window. When your parents ask what happened, you have two options, you blame it on the dog or you confess that it was you who broke it. It is the same with capitalism. You can choose to study, work hard, and try your best, in which case you have high chances of succeeding and reaching your dreams. But if you don't, it is easier to blame it on others than to take responsibility.

Only true grown-ups can take responsibility for the consequences of their actions because it takes courage to do so.

Grown-ups pick the hard path: taking responsibility.
It's always easier to blame others.

That is why you see the world today as "upside down". Because socialists lost to capitalism, their obsession is to destroy freedom, because even though capitalism has its problems, of course, it is far superior to socialism. That is why socialists applaud when women are forced to be covered from head to toe in some cultures. That is why socialists celebrate when someone burns the national flag, which stands for patriotism and unity. That is why socialists tell men that they can be women and women can be men. That is the way in which socialists try to convince others that nobody has to grow up and take control of their lives. And that is why socialists support censorship, immorality, and violence even in universities, the very places where one is supposed to learn how to think, debate different ideas, and mature. Socialism is like extending childhood (irresponsibility) forever. It is very comfortable because, like in the socialist paradise, there is always someone else to blame.

The socialist world is upside down:
bad is good and right is wrong.

By dividing people into "identity groups", the socialists made everything about power struggles. And, once again, like 100 years ago, they aspire to make everybody identical, like little robots with the same opinions, dreams, thoughts, and actions. By splitting people into tribes, the socialists made it difficult for people to work together in order to make their dreams come true. And, most importantly, they created a generation of people who prefer to blame everything on others instead of taking responsibility for themselves. Just like the times when the gulags started.

In socialism what matters isn't the individual
but the group. All identical.
like a group of perfect, identical snowflakes.

100 years later the world is about to see socialism happen again. And that is a sad thing because, as demonstrated, socialism gives way to communism and then oppression, death, and poverty. Everybody will be equally miserable and violence will return against those who dare to think differently. People will not worry about making decisions because decisions will be made for them by the big government. Everything will be owned by everybody and, therefore, nobody will take responsibility for anything … including their own life.

- Mom, why is everything so good? —asked little Charlie.
- Because we are equal and the government
takes care of us, little Chuck—dad replied
- Can I be a girl and play with fire?
- Yeah, whatever...

VISIT NOW!
www.chihuahua.dog

CHECK OUT OUR UPCOMING CHILDREN'S BOOKS:
"MUM, AM I A GIRL OR A BOY?"
"SHUT UP! I AM DEFENDING FREE SPEECH"
"I'M 6 AND I DON'T WANT TO MARRY THAT OLD MAN"

Made in United States
Troutdale, OR
03/11/2024